Prison Segmentation For Safety,

And Sanity, Security, Peace & Space

Reverend Mike Wanner

Copyright

August 11, 2017

Reverend Mike Wanner

Selected Images Used by License

Table Of Contents

1 - Why I am Writing This Book _____ 5
2 - The Intensity of Density _____ 9
3 - Space Segmentation _____ 10
4 - Space Use & Safety _____ 11
5 - Space Can Help Reduce Stress _____ 12
6 - How Can Space Be Used Differently? _____ 13
7 - Initial Analysis _____ 14
8 - Space Use Goals _____ 15
9 - Essential Service In the Segments _____ 16
10 - Why We Have What We Have _____ 17
11 - We All Can Do a Lot More _____ 18
12 - Changing Your Mind Changes A Lot _____ 19
13 - Kind People Can Be Vulnerable _____ 20
14 - How Would Segmentation Work _____ 21
15 - How Could Space be Utilized? _____ 23
16 - What Would Prisoners Suggest? _____ 24
17 - "Acknowledging the Invitation" _____ 26
18 - Segmentation Could Take Many Forms _____ 27
19 - Rehabilitation _____ 28
20 - Thank You _____ 29
21 - Don't Worry Ever _____ 30
22 - Resource Books _____ 31
23 - Angels Please Prayers _____ 33
24 - Private Channeling _____ 34
25 - Reverend Mike Wanner _____ 35

Introduction

Some sources report that in America alone there are more than 2.3 million people in jail.

All the intellect in all those residents may not be used well because the owners of the brains are incarcerated, and a major issue for them may well be their safety.

I, like most people, was oblivious to that fact until I was invited to look into it. I started channeling Angel Raphael in 2013 and began releasing little message sets as they came through.

In message set 16 of the Angel Raphael Speaks Series there was a message that has remained floating in my head since as topic for my writing.

The message I resisted was an invitation to visit jail energetically. Here is that message –

"I asked Mike to Step into Prison Energetically

I have asked Mike to get the address and location within a prison of a designated space so he can visit energetically and receive feedback for us to consider. Whether he will have time, interest or opportunity to do this will be interesting to see. As he writes this, he is not thrilled with the idea. We are already consuming a lot of his time." ARS16

1 - I am Writing This Book Because

I embraced the invitation in 2016. So far, The Angel Raphael prodding has had me publish the following books related to prisons:

1. *Angel Raphael Speaks Volume 4: Angels, Addicts, Alcoholics & Prisoners - Oh Yeah!*
2. *Angel Raphael Speaks Volume 5: Prisoners Caring for Alcoholics - Australia In Miniature   Projects Intro*
3. *Angel Raphael Speaks Volume 6: Prisoners Caring for Addicts - Australia In Miniature For   Addicts*
4. *Prison Jobs Now: Providing Care For Addicts And Alcoholics*
5. *Angel Raphael Speaks - Prisons (A Kindle only book -2013)*
6. *Contained Care Communities: Concept*
7. *Australia In Miniature*
8. *Prison Possibilities Dialogue Series: Concept*
9. *Prison Possibilities Dialogue Series: Volume 2 Dialogues*
10. *Prison Possibilities Dialogue Series: Volume 3 Dialogues*
11. *Prison Possibilities Dialogue Series: Volume 4 Dialogues*
12. *Prison Possibilities Dialogue Series: Volume 5 Dialogues*
13. *Prison Possibilities Voluntary Exile: Concept*
14. *Prison Possibilities Correction Coaches: Concept*
15. *Prison Possibilities for Mexicans: Is A Boat Better than A Wall?*
16. *Prison Possibilities Family Time: A Reason to Thrive!*
17. *Prison Genius Pool: "So Much Genius In Jail."*
18. *Prison Possibilities Access Systems: Prisoner Access by Request*
19. *Prisoner's Lawyers Can Save The American Economy: Make A Buck Doing It & Be Thanked!*

20. *Prisoner Family Talks, Days, Stays & Vacations: Connecting Helps Healing*
21. *Prisoner Writing Projects: Write To Heal, Start Over & Reconnect*
22. *Prison Cell Clearing & Blessing: Clear Entities, Chase Ghosts, and & Create Sacred Space*
23. *Prisoner Professors: Show You Are Aware Create Change With Care*
24. *Prison Reiki? Maybe Someday? A Gateway To Help Heal Prisons & America?*
25. *Judges and An Angel Rule On Possibilities: We Can Cut Sentences & Prison Costs*
26. *Ideas For Prison Wardens: Leadership Is Not Easy*
27. *Solitary Community: Could Community Support Cut Costs and Issues?*
28. *Prisoner Projects Communication Teams: Communications Can Change Lives*
29. *Motivating & Empowering Prisoners? Invite Prisoners To Find Their Motivation & Their Future*

This book continues to carry the potential for rethinking that can help to reduce incarceration to those who we need to have there.

I want to trigger mindset shifts in the prisoners as well as employees and the community. We need a lot more Objective Productive Dialogues about Enhancing the lives of Prison Employees, Prisoners, Taxpayers and the Families of Each of these groups.

As I have been writing my books on Prisons, the complexity of the process has amazed me. I have some ideas of ways that might help, but I surrender to guidance.

My guidance suggests that we need a lot of creativity. Open minds on both sides of every issue can make great strides.

Open-mindedness is a real key point as closed minds may be one of the leading causes of the negativity that exists. Consider any argument that you ever had and remember that accommodation will usually follow a gesture of respect.

My perspective has been hard to achieve, but there seem to be some more dialogues that I would like to share:

1. Understanding the costs of Prisons is complicated, and states and programs have so many variables that most folks will be lost as I have been.

2. The humanity is difficult to balance because just like prison costs are difficult to measure, so are the human factors.

3. Change is needed to create balance and accountability so that fiscal responsibility is comparable between states, regions, and facilities.

4. The negative influence of trendy cultural shifts is not helping to achieve reasonable options.

5. Answers will not be simple or quick.

6. Creativity will be key to balance.

7. Those who care could share and communicate.

8. Uninvolved citizens do not help,

9. Voters have the power to change everything by their choices.

10. The answers will not come from someone who does not care so if you care then you just might want to get active in the American Political System.

The Intensity Of Density Can Cause Enormous Stress

Space Segmentation Could Be A Stress Diffuser

4 - Space Use & Safety

The ideas that I put forth may have little to offer the residents and staff members at your particular location as all facilities are different. I am hopeful that many prisoners will benefit, so that is why I am writing.

The stories and pictures of incarceration that are seen on the outside may be inaccurate, and it may be that some facilities have reasonable space for all residents and staff members. I hope space is there for you or those you love.

Like so many activities there seem to be one major way of thinking and that may be how organizations set up in what seems like a logical flow. I do not think there is only one way that can make sense and me especially that original thought and analysis can benefit many prisoners and prison staff.

If you have adequate room in your facility, then you need not read much further. If on the other hand, congestion of activities and people are bothersome then I invite you to continue reading.

It is normal for human beings to require a certain amount of private space which will vary with each person. Some people like being close together in situations.

I would not think that prison is a situation where people generally would like to be close. Oddly, there seems to be a level of emotional distance which happens naturally as a result of the dense use of space which can create emotional disconnects from normal behavior outside the walls.

5 - Space Can Help Reduce Stress

Prisoners can be influenced by the space available to them. Space Density can be stifling while spaciousness can promote creativity and peaceful co-existence.

True as that statement is, there is a limit to the space available. The point that I would raise again, already, still is the need for creativity and thinking outside the box about the allocation and use of the space available.

There can be a reality of creative thought that can change utility and increase benefit. The stakes are high in prison, for the prisons, the prisoners, the prison staff's families, the prisoner's families, the taxpayer and their families, the government agencies, the states and municipalities, the national government and our society as a whole.

We can change the system, and we will but the big question is – "How many lives will be un-optimized by any chaos that exists until we start the necessary changes?" We are all in the boat, and it is sinking.

I can almost hear the voices saying that the problem does not affect me and my answer to that is BSSS (Bull Stinky Solid Stuff).

All taxpayers are affected by the costs of prisons. All citizens are worthy of as much freedom as their behavior allows.

6 - How Can Space Be Used Differently?

Earlier I wrote a Prison book titled *Prison Possibilities Access Systems: Prisoner Access by Request.* That book started a discussion about access to space and how prisoners can flow through that space.

I would encourage many conversations about Safety, Sanity, Security, Peace & Space use. The objective of the conversations would be about how to use space more wisely.

If we begin to think of prisons as a 24-hour facility, we can then believe that certain areas could be progressively developed to be better utilized. Hospitals and Airports have many functions going on around the clock, and these different shifts rarely get in the way of each other.

With the right motivations and access controls, we could begin to progressively refit out facilities to be much safer, much more secure, much more prisoner friendly, much more prison staff friendly, much less stressful and much more peaceful.

We could coincidentally reduce prison conflicts, increase correction officers safety, reduce medical costs incidental to conflicts, reduce lost corrections officer's time caused by being hurt scuffling with prisoners.

7 - Initial Analysis

Early on at no expense, we can begin to look at the occupancy times for sections of the facility.

We need to know based on the programs in place, the total utilization of the primary function areas of the facility.

Next, we need to know all incidental times that prisoners who perform services are using those primary function areas to prepare for the major services that they provide.

Next, we need to know All the Primary Function areas that have blocks of time that are unavailable for prisoner access.

Next, we need to know the lesser used areas of the prison and all the blocks of time that those areas are empty of prisoners and how long those blocks of time are.

Next, we will need to know all the times when the cell blocks that prisoners sleep in are empty and not accessible to the prisoners.

Next, we need to look at the service areas and find all the service area space that is empty for periods of time and how long those periods are and what options might be possible for all the open space with new occupancy plans.

8 - Space Use Goals

Over time and in a progressive way that avoids capital costs, space can be reallocated to align use with enhanced function.

Where possible, facilities can endeavor to create a B shift and or a C Shift that will offer great new freedom to prisoners to select patterns or tracks of new segmentation within the facility.

Many stories share some unplanned segmentation of groups of inmates who group themselves based on ethnic or cultural orientations. The concept shared here is not organized to work against those choices of alignment by prisoners interests but to increase freedom and space.

This concept should prove helpful to all prisoners and staff by spreading out the residents and allowing more space per prisoner at many times.

Each facility that chooses to make some adjustments based on this idea could receive incidental security benefit by having residents spread throughout the facility around the clock.

Prisons that make some changes based on this idea could increase prisoner safety benefit by having residents spread throughout the institution at optimal times to avoid overcrowding.

Management that chooses to make some adjustments based on this idea could have stress reduction throughout, and prisoners who are at higher risk may be more easily separated from potential conflicts with others.

9 - Essential Service In the Segments

Planning will be needed to provide all required benefits to all prisoners, and that will have to be planned before any changes.

While space use is important, so are the full range of rights and privileges for each prisoner.

Of course, prisoners could be returned to the general population whenever necessary for prison operations.

The hope with this system would be the benefit of additional space and freedom which could ultimately be instrumental in making a case for more creative changes to the institutional control systems within the system.

The simplest way to move forward can be the teamwork that seems lacking in prison. Ideally, we can move towards a scenario where the underprivileged of yesterday can begin to become the insurers of privileges for those who without their efforts would be doomed to the injustices of the past.

Teamwork and justice and freedom while the goals of the Formation of this country may have been lost to many. Let us now use the devastation of incarceration to identify and change the problems of yesteryear and create a new bounty of possibilities now. Let us all seek peace as we build on the foundation of freedom that has nurtured our predecessors in the country that we treasure.

10 - Why We Have What We Have

What we have is survival positions based on alignment with options that were the best available when chosen. What we need is an opportunity for everything to be better for everyone who lives, works, or pays for prison. That means all citizens everywhere, and it includes many of the free citizens who have been denied services because too much has already been spent on old fashioned ineffective processes.

The collective skills that help us cope with what is may be terrible options that serve no one and deteriorate our faith in our fellow human beings. We have all seen stories of questioned prison performance.

I challenge every reader to offer their genius to help serve the America that we love. We need optimal prison options.

We need deliberate frugal ideas that carry the seeds of change to every prison everywhere in the country. Caution is necessary to avoid radical increases in prison costs as we increase efficiency.

We need to stop paying huge sums of money for processes and perspectives that deny human dignity and nurture evil. We need to reassess, reorganize, reinvent and reinvigorate.

We cannot change when we view change as impossible. We need to think possibility and persistence on a reasoned, deliberate path to improving outcomes within institutions that have stopped deteriorating and are reversing course.

11 - We All Can Do a Lot More

We can do a lot more with a lot less. We can grow teamwork and tenacity, and we can upscale the lives of all who help us.

Helping each other is the key to survive and thrive in a free society. Prison creates a ceiling to freedom but no limit to stress, anxiety, and confusion.

We can break through limitations if we have enough motivation and support. We can focus our collective energies in new ways that will create opportunities for success for us all.

Prison residents and staff can each enhance the lives of each other if they can discipline themselves enough to listen and consider. The key to unlocking success is understanding the needs of each other and gifting others with kindness.

Life is like the story of a perspective of heaven and hell. I know not the author or I would give credit.

The story shows the same picture of a place of bounty where all sit at a table of opportunity epitomized by luscious fruit and vegetables and delicacies of all kinds. The problem in both pictures is that the utensils are attached to the hands of those at the table in a way that makes it impossible for each person to feed themselves.

Hell has all at the table starving as they struggle to get nourishment. Heaven has all people thriving because they each take turns in feeding each other. Which table will you choose? You may have chosen, but you can change your mind.

12 - Changing Your Mind Changes A Lot

Your mind can filter things out or allow them into your life. It would be my recommendation that you begin to reassess the choices of the past that set the limits of what you have now.

You are a powerful being even if you have been broken by your life circumstances or any of the events that occurred since your birth. The simple little powerful tool that can help you begin a new journey of personal discovery is simply kindness.

Be kind first to yourself and soothe the pain that you know. Next look metaphorically for the burrs under your saddle that impact on the horse you ride.

As you treat yourself far more kindly and spread the impact of your kindness to other beings on the planet, your state of being will metamorphize into a potential that you have not even dreamed possible. That new vision of possibility can be a bit much, and it can take you into a feeling of vulnerability that is new and fresh and scary.

While that may sound ominous, the reality is that it may simply be an unknown quantity that you can assess, evaluate and develop into a future that you might like.

13 - Kind People Can Be Vulnerable

Transitions in life are a great opportunity but also have a vulnerability. Prisons are not exactly user-friendly so caution and deliberation would be wise if you are considering changes.

Prison segmentation for safety may help present opportunities that can grow into feelings that allow growth. One must be aware, however, that the segmentation could cease during changing circumstances or unrest within a facility so it may be wise to study judiciously before taking any stands that could backfire on you.

One program may not change the real world but could offer opportunities that could be helpful. Persistence is important to the quality of your tomorrows, but caution is needed to avoid risks that diligence could prevent.

Please pursue better tomorrows and prevent any challenges you might encounter if you put others down in the process. Kindness is needed toward those of your past so that every possible seed of resentment withers and does not jeopardize your hard work.

If segmentation works for you and allows you to align with new opportunities, appreciation for all who made the segmentation possible can help you keep the benefits and encourage the spreading of the good start. Your continued success will be contingent on you showing the universe that you have raised your vibration to a level that resonates with higher vibrational thinking and manifestation. Any return to selfish behavior can be a seed for a future failure.

14 - How Would Segmentation Work?

Over time and in a progressive way that avoids capital costs, space can be reallocated to align utility with enhanced function. I used the idea of shifts that hospitals and airports use above to begin an example of timed functionality.

The idea is to provide opportunities to spread people out and improve possibilities for all. For most of the residents, things could stay pretty similar for awhile unless someone wanted to step up and out on a path of making things better for everybody.

Every great accomplishment starts with unusual ideas of things or new uses for different applications. Inventors of all kinds and visionaries go through a lot to bring us breakthroughs and are frequently not well rewarded.

Prisoners may have a more immediate reward in that the creation of a segmentation proposal could be solely in the use of thinking and dreaming and bringing alive faith or hope even if the experience is fleeting. Prison may be off-putting boring to many, and that may have something to do with the playground like competitions that can trigger trouble.

Even brain surgeons can find life boring when they are only doing the same things the same way in the same place every day just like the day before. Life is worth living when it is vibrant and fresh and dynamic and startlingly unpredictable.

Have you ever noticed that eating the same thing over and over again is boring? Even gourmet restaurants can be boring when it is always same and same again.

Life is vibrationally stimulated by new activities. When your sports team comes to your neighborhood and has tryouts for the kids, there becomes a new life of purpose that changes the vibrancy and joy of those who see it manifest.

Segmentation can allow diversity of many things to enhance the possibilities for the conceptualizing of a whole series of potentials that never before existed for any prisoners.

Segmentation can promote hope and potential and allow enough space for the manifestation of new life in the brains of old bodies. New thoughts can breed new realities that can eventually manifest into new good for many.

15 - How Could Space be Utilized?

Over time and in a progressive way that avoids capital costs, space can be evaluated to find blocks of time that can be reallocated to find new utility and enhanced function. I used the idea of shifts in hospitals and airports above to begin an example of timed functionality.

Hospitals usually have three shifts, and they may be something like 7 AM -11 PM, and 11 PM - 7 AM and 7 AM – 11 PM. A little later, a little earlier matters not but the mission is the determining factor.

Prisons also could vary depending on their priorities. The prime benefit for prison segmentation could likely be adding the benefit of perceiving more space per prisoner when there is no more physical space in the existing building.

Spaciousness can help with feelings of peace and freedom and personal power. Overcrowding can contribute to feelings of frustration, resentment, and anger.

Spaciousness can enhance cooperation and pleasantness. Being pleasant makes things easier for everybody and avoids flare-ups that could be costly in personal terms and facility function.

Even little bits of added spaciousness can lower the stress for everybody and may lead to better cooperation in many things. I do not have an ultimate plan for how this all could manifest, but just the idea of additional space may help prisoners in an overcrowded facility for a long-term to begin to think of possibilities.

16 - What Would Prisoners Suggest?

Prisoners do not get a lot of opportunities to express themselves in meaningful positive ways. I have previously written a few books about Prisoners creating Dialogues which could be helpful, but that effort could be influenced or stifled by many things.

Please note that this approach is positive and not pushing against as I sincerely believe that teamwork is the answer to the prison situation.

Asking prisoners for positive ideas may be a tree of possibility that can bear fruit for all to enjoy.

Here is the Introduction to the Dialogue Concept-

"Introduction

I invite every reader to consider publishing a simple 200-word article about an idea that has the capability to be the seed of a positive perspective shift for the readers of it. This invitation is not to vent or blame. I encourage you to publish the articles yourself and submit to news media and politicians and also send them to me at ReverendMikeWanner@aol.com if you would like me to consider your possibilities for publication.

I invite you to share your wisdom as a seed for those who read your idea. You could intend that they will be able to focus their energy in a way that will prepare your idea seed to grow and help them and others.

The messages could help heal, release, seed, process, understand, rethink, conceptualize, organize and otherwise analyze the who, what, when, where, how and why of an event. Understanding things can allow new perspectives of the ways that everything and everyone fit into the grand scheme of things.

Life is an experience, and it has a timeline for us all. While you are here on earth, you can stay stuck in what is as time ticks away, and your life dissipates. You could also consider changing the what is.

There is nothing wrong with being traditional. A great path is to pursue the change in a responsible way so that there are no mistakes that set up new problems. The invitation is to learn and study and change what all agree to change."

The Dialogue process could be very effective if applied to conversations about segmentation. I have posted the Invitation To Dialogue in Chapter 15 below.

17 - "Acknowledging the Invitation."
{From Chapter 3 of *Prison Possibilities Dialogue Series: Concept*}

"The way to acknowledge the invitation is to respond to or create a Titled page outlining the premise of your title so that new discussions or responses can be submitted to enhance or counter the initial report. Brevity and clarity of thought are paramount.

There are so many variables that we need to triage thought somewhat and group areas that need action. Pivotal to this effort will be the avoidance of blame because the evolution of what now exists is not assignable as participants over the years were acting in response to implementation of the best of limited options and we need not waste more money that does not help current citizens.

Participation is invited to both create and respond to the ideas that are needed to bring change that can impact the lives of those individuals (and their families) who live or work in prison and those who are influenced by the shortage of government funds because of the money spent on prisons.

Responses submitted to me are invited in a particular format to make certain that the responses are similar enough to be easily compared and organized. I hope to be able to publish responses in sufficient numbers to make a difference.

The desired format is a single Page Configuration >200 words <220 Words, in a 6 x 9 book format with all .5 margins, Title Font 20 Pt. Times New Roman, Body Font 14 Pt. Times New Roman. Adherence to the desired format will go a long way to simplify the process for me. Thank You."

18 - Segmentation Could Take Many Forms

The use of segmentation can evolve to a kind of respite from the prison norm that allows for a peaceful time out where one can separate from their everyday associations and allow their mind to settle down and find some privacy, peace, and sanity.

Citizens in much less stressful situations need a break or mental health day. Prisoners also could benefit from reassessing the day to day grind.

I have some further ideas about the way segmentation can help, but for now, I would love to see what ideas prisoners can share that might catch fire and help the whole community

I would suggest to all that starting with a non-toxic mindset will be helpful to your success. Forgiveness of others can ratchet up your power to a new level of potential.

Segmentation can be a privilege that all disciplined residents could benefit from when they share ideas and peace and cooperation.

I would enjoy seeing Dialogues of potentials for:
- One night segmentation
- Two-night segmentation
- One week segmentations
- Writers segmentations
- Efficiency segmentations
- Security segmentations
- Safety segmentations
- Creativity segmentations

19 - Rehabilitation

A goal that some folks expect of incarceration is rehabilitation. I hear little about successes in that pursuit but would be delighted to hear of new potentials for that to happen.

I believe that success is more likely if there can be more open-minded, creative thought applied to everything related to prisons and jails and other parts of the legal system.

There seem to be opposing positions on each side of every issue, and I feel that tendency on both the side of administration and the side that is sensitive to the incarcerated. I suggest to both points of view that there is needed a side to all things that minimize opposition and promote team efforts to finesse new ideas that benefit all the interested parties which would include the Prisons, the Prisoners and especially the taxpayers.

All three interests are diminished by opposition by anybody to anything. Interestingly, I see greater value in saying and doing nothing than there is in opposing anything suggested by anybody.

Fractional progress can be much more efficient than absolute objection. If all parties agree on the part of an idea, then we have real progress.

With any luck in prison, Congress may adopt the process and America can thrive. Prisons and Prisoners and taxpayers can lead the way. My question is – Will You?

20 - Thank You

For Considering These Ideas

21 - Don't Worry Ever

Ever

It Does Not Help Prayer Still Does!

22 - Resource Books

Distant Healing Sessions (or Join Mail List) – Write To mikewann@voicenet.com

Books by Rev. Mike at www.Amazon.com

Veterans Healing Six Pack
1. *Trauma Healing Options for VA Hospitals: Help for Veterans to Own Their Healing and their future.*
2. *Trauma Healing Action Steps for Veterans: Help to Start Healing*
3. *Trauma Healing Action Steps for Veterans: Empowerment*
4. *Trauma Healing Action Steps for Veterans: Forgiveness*
5. *Trauma Healing Action Steps for Veterans: Thought Freedom*
6. *Tea For Veterans: Welcome One Home*

PTSD Power Pack:
1. The PTSD Project: Turn Pain To Power
2. PTSD & Soul Retrieval: Putting One Back Together
3. PTSD & The Purple PAD: Calling all Scientists and PTSD Patients

Angel Raphael Speaks Volume 1: Take Courage! God Has Healing in Store for You!
Angel Raphael Speaks Volume 2: Take Courage! God Has Healing in Store for You!
Angel Raphael Speaks Volume 3: Take Courage! God Has Healing in Store for You!
Angel Raphael Speaks Volume 4: Angels, Addicts, Alcoholics & Prisoners – Oh Yeah!
Angel Raphael Speaks Volume 5: Prisoners Caring for Alcoholics - Australia In Miniature Projects Intro
Angel Raphael Speaks Volume 6: Prisoners Caring for Addicts - Australia In Miniature For Addicts
Reiki Journaling from Japan
Reiki Is Alive: God's Great Gift
Four Parts to Healing
Distant Healing: We Are All Connected
Stress Release Energy Work: How To Cope
Does Reiki Love Heal Cancer?
Group Consciousness
Salute To Philadelphia VA Medical Center: Thank You
Reiki Transcript for Reiki 2 & 3 Channels: Dr. Usui Is That You?
God Bless Kindle & Amazon
Puppies Are Different From People
If Your Dog Dies
Toy Guns Are Obsolete

Great Spirit Made Children With Red Skin: AND
The Cage of Fear: Is Not Locked
God Made Children Red, Yellow, Brown, Black & White: Greet Each Child With Kindness
Emergency Medical Kindness In The Cradle Of Liberty: Big City - Cracked Bell
Angels Are Always Around Addicts and Addicts: Help Is Near Now! Invite It In!
Angels Are Always Around Addicts and Alcoholics: Volume 2 - Tools To Help Re-Light Your Life
Prison Jobs Now: Providing Care For Addicts And Addicts
Controlled Care Communities Concept
Prison Possibilities Dialogue Series: Concept
Prison Possibilities Dialogue Series: Volume 2, 3, 4, 5 Dialogues
Prison Possibilities Voluntary Exile
Prison Possibilities Corrections Coaches
Prison Possibilities For Mexicans: Is A Boat Better Than A Wall?
Prison Possibilities Family Time: A Reason to Thrive!
Prison Genius Pool: "So Much Genius In Jail."
Prison Possibilities Access Control: Prisoner Access by Request
Prisoner's Lawyers Can Save The American Economy: Make A Buck Doing It & Be Thanked!
Prisoner Family Talks, Days, Stays & Vacations: Connecting Helps Healing
Prisoner Writing Projects: Write To Heal, Start Over & Reconnect
Prison Cell Clearing & Blessing: Clear Entities, Chase Ghosts, and & Create Sacred Space
Prisoner Professors: Show You Are Aware Create Change With Care
Prison Reiki? Maybe Someday? A Gateway To Help Heal Prisons & America?
Judges and An Angel Rule On Possibilities: We Can Cut Sentences & Prison Costs
Ideas For Prison Wardens: Leadership Is Not Easy
Solitary Community: Could Community Support Cut Costs and Issues?

Little Books at Kindle.com by Rev. Mike:
English Medical History Questionnaire For Non-English Speakers
English Language Helper For Non-English Speakers
Wise Wonderful Women Are The Well Of The Family
Answers for Test & Research: Dowsing Power
Crisis? Reiki! Baby? Reiki!
Bible References For Healing
Angel Raphael Speaks – Prisons
Angel Raphael Speaks – Veterans
The Saint Off Interstate 95

23 - Angels Please Prayers

Addict's

Angels of Healing Selected
Help Me to Stay Directed
Come To Me From The Sky
I Am Ready to Succeed Not Try
If I Don't Invite You In
I Might Not Win
I Have Been Lost For Too Long
Help Me To Stay Strong

Alcoholic's

Angels of Healing On High
Help Me to Stay Dry
Come To Me From The Sky
I Am Ready to Succeed Not Try
If I Don't Invite You In
I Might Not Win
I Have Been Lost For Too Long
Help Me To Stay Strong

From

24 - Private Channeling

Angel Raphael Speaks a series of free messages that are channeled through Reverend Mike Wanner for the Highest good and Highest Healing of all concerned.

Many questions arise about Reverend Mike doing private channeling, and he does help with that so e-mail him.

Reverend Mike is available worldwide as a psychic channel, emotional release facilitator, spiritual energy practitioner & teacher, and public speaker. He looks forward to meeting you soon!

Email - mikewann@voicenet.com 215-342-1270 PRIVATE SPIRITUAL READINGS/channelings or Spiritual Healing Sessions: Telephone or in person. Rev. Mike is available for private, one-on-one intuitive sessions with you, his Guide Family, and your Guides. He helps by offering clarity on emotional situations about your life, your purpose, your spirituality, and the release of stuffed emotions and cellular memory.
Connect to the love of your Guides today!
Contact Rev. Mike for an appointment.
Sessions available:
Spiritual Readings
Angel Channeling
Distant Reiki Healing
Distant Clearing of Stuffed Emotions
Distant Clearing Cellular Memory
Distant Clearing Energy Blockages
Distant Clearing of the Chakras
Customized needs
Mastermind dowsing responses to yes/no direction finding questions.

Rev. Mike is a facilitator of healing. He brings you and the Divine together so that you can align with the Divine and have a great time and a great life. All healing is between you and God, as it should be. Go ahead and start without Rev. Mike. Visit his prayer site http://www.Create-A-Prayer.com. Take the first step NOW.

25 - Reverend Mike Wanner

Rev. Mike Wanner started his Metaphysical and Ministerial studies with Reiki in 1993 and had studied seven styles of Reiki in the U.S., Japan, Canada, Denmark and Australia. He is certified to teach. He became certified to teach Integrated Energy Therapy in 1999 and co-taught the first IET class of the new Millennium. Mike began dowsing in 2001.

Ordained as a Metaphysical Minister of the International Metaphysical Ministry and an Interfaith Minister of the Circle of Miracles Ministry, Rev. Mike practices and teaches spiritual energy therapies in the Philadelphia Area.

Rev. Mike holds ministerial degrees from the University of Metaphysics and the University of Sedona. He is a Pastoral Care Associate of Aria - Frankford Hospital. He taught at the National Academy of Massage Therapy and Health Sciences.

Rev. Mike was a faculty member of the Medical Mission Sister's Center for Human Integration's School of Integrated Body/Mind Therapies in Fox Chase, Philadelphia, PA for twelve years.

Rev. Mike is licensed by the teaching of Intuitional Metaphysics to practice Spiritual Healing and Scientific Prayer. Mike is also a Prayer therapist.

Rev. Mike was elected in 2007 to the status of "Fellow of the American Institute of Stress."

In 2008, Rev. Mike became a practitioner of Coincidental Recognition as he incorporated the CoRe System into his spiritual healing practice.

In 2009, Rev. Mike trademarked a new healing process called Quantum Quatro! Subtle Energy System Support®.

In 2011, Rev. Mike joined the outreach program known as the Health Advantage Group.

In 2012, Rev. Mike became a Certified Professional Coach by The Master Coaching Academy and Joined the Personal Empowerment Group.

Before his Metaphysical, Ministerial and Coaching studies, Rev. Mike worked for Sears Roebuck and Co. while in High School and after graduation, until he joined the U. S. Air Force in 1965. He returned to Sears from Vietnam in 1969 and stayed until 1978. His final Sears assignment was as an efficiency expert in Methods - Operational Research and Development.

He volunteered with Burholme Emergency Medical Services from 1969 and is still a Life Member and Board of Directors Member. He started a private ambulance company in 1975 and worked professionally in the field until 2001 when he devoted his full attention to real estate investing, healing, coaching, and writing.

www.ingramcontent.com/pod-product-compliance
Lightning Source LLC
Chambersburg PA
CBHW071203240526
45470CB00017B/1248